Comma Fork
Moving Parts

Also by Ted Greenwald:

Clearview / LIE (United Artists, 2011)
3 (Cuneiform Press, 2008)
Permanent Record (LRL, 2008)
In Your Dreams (BlazeVox, 2008)
Two Wrongs (Cuneiform Press, 2007) with Hal Saulson
The Up and Up (Atelos, 2004)
Jumping the Line (Roof Books, 1999)
Something, She's Dead (MEB/PNY, 1999)
More Than All (Tongue to Boot, 1999) with Michael Gottlieb
Acme Down (1999) with Abby Greenwald
You Go Through (Case Books, 1992)
Looks Like I'm Walking (Case Books, 1991)
Poker Blues (1991) video in collaboration with Les Levine
Word of Mouth (Sun and Moon, 1986)
Exit the Face (Museum of Modern Art, 1982) with Richard Bosman
Young and Restless (Case Books, 1982) with George Schneeman
Smile (Tuumba, 1981)
Use No Hooks (Asylum's Press, 1980)
Common Sense (L Publications, 1979)
Licorice Chronicles (Kulchur Foundation, 1979)
You Bet! (This, 1978)
Native Land (Titanic Books, 1977)
The Life (Big Sky Books, 1975)
Miami (Doones Press, 1975)
Makes Sense (Angel Hair, 1975)
The New Money (Sand Project Press, 1973)
Making a Living (Adventures in Poetry, 1973)
Blink (Buffalo Press, 1972)
Somewhere in Ho (Buffalo Press, 1972) with Ed. Baynard
No Eating (Blue Pig, 1971)
Short Sleeves (Buffalo Press, 1970)
Lapstrake (Lines, 1965)

COMMA FORK
MOVING PARTS

Ted Greenwald

BlazeVox Books

ISBN: 978-1-60964-096-5
LCCN: 2012938516

Thanks to Charles Bernstein, Miles Champion,
Geoffrey Gatza, Kyle Schlesinger and Brandelyn Wiser.

Some of these poems appeared in *Mimeo Mimeo, Sal
Mimeo* and *The Recluse*.

CONTENTS

COMMA FORK

for Anne and Donald

Read in a magazine
Lo mein
Ohmigod

I say, *shit*
He say, *yeah*
Come here yesterday

Ate there once
With Carol
You know Carol

If you like pass encore
Echo own nothing count blessing wounds
Where everybody repeat after math

Echo own nothing be before
No idea road repeat after math
Where everybody pass encore

                    TED GREENWALD

Slip into a slinky
Descending a staircase
I'm a I'm a I'm a

Age inside out
We aim to microwave
Open back car

Try being Mi Mi
Defenestrate crazy glaze
Lazy-boid days

Early on, for me, national interest fever
Light under bushel passing for vehicle
Am *that idiot* officials say suggestion

Light under bushel good grasp singalong
Break into line officials say suggestion
Am *that idiot* national interest fever

                                        TED GREENWALD

Dismantle mental dollars
Suppose the next month
Toddle along in my wrecker

Put the hook in the rain
Come to right places
Money particles dust lights

Ex-girlfriends walks by
My bad, it's grandkids
But, but, memento more me

Mark these words body of owner
Vote dayglo work out of
Come clean be forgot about

Vote dayglo dropping off
House up sold on be forgot about
Come clean body of owner

                                        TED GREENWALD

A lot's traffic
Cross mind
Crossing legs

Doublecross the mind
Double yellow lines
Pass where broke

Triple cross
Coda in english
Brights

Daily double thinkling twice
As with all twins nature seconds
Leg scratches head mustard onions

As with all twins if ah so
Second take mustard onions
Leg scratches head thinkling twice

                              TED GREENWALD

Your own lights
Run together
You run the lights

Turn towards
You run the table
Wards off, that's snow

Your differs drift
They so *huh*
They do so *huh*

Leave parts unknown reverse engineer
Empty head into map go goat
Prayer rug kill said bridge

Empty head into map be clear, no blam
Pour heart out said bridge
Prayer rug kill reverse engineer

                                        TED GREENWALD

Continue on through
None other than
It's the head yoyo

Nod head
Once for *yes*   Twice
Write in pseudo

Blue pseudo shoes
Speak kindly of
And not first time

Deep in parkest heart keep inside
Drink from portable oven, winter comes early
Ashen faces turn ashes squirrel away

Drink from portable oven spring in sum
Lost mine emeralds squirrel away
Ashen faces turn ashes keep inside

                    TED GREENWALD

As is clearly snows
The speaker engraves
Close to grammar

As it clearly snows
The speaker hews
Create whole cloth

Gets warmer
Hmm really
Really hot

Child calls name still night
Too talks eyes only
Slips by say so different eyes on

Too talks with all your might
Tell again different eyes on
Slips by say so still night

TED GREENWALD

Snapshot accident
As dead as
Fond favorite letters

Heads from behind
Ass from hole in ground
The sky seeps

Possibilities endless Sue-ish
You have a friend
Shake *hi* the dog's paw

Paper covers rock turn off when leaves
Kit science evolves wangle finger invite
Knife cuts air current events mist

Kit science evolves history delight
Verbal elementary school current events mist
Knife cuts air turn off when leaves

 TED GREENWALD

Crush rehab like a copse
We sway to the birches
It's winter in another country

Light pre-seeds each meadow
Strangers appear as smoke
A la mode transport carry the one

Return from work return calls
Unfamiliar number jumps
Windy with today snow

Handwriting as belongings call for cuts
Describe as everyone says positions' accord
Next year openers streetwise otherwise

Describe as everyone says country playing field
Miss baby tooth streetwise otherwise
Next year openers calls for cuts

                    TED GREENWALD

Mind changes
Clothes change
Straight drop down

As original
Seems
Look right

Road's miniscue
Fever cartoon
Oncoming radiator

Level scrutiny free offer autographs
Bare science wear shanties
Nooses off cinderblock lead cheers

Bare science unless phys contact
Welcome to black sites lead cheers
Nooses off cinderblock free offer autographs

                    TED GREENWALD

Vehicles and their people
Traffic emends rush hour
Pull into own plaza

A hand exits window
Brief come hitherish, you toll
No questions, don't ask

Shift lanes, set up EXIT
Take, shift follow lane
Baby is on its baby way

Airline fish fly audit nothings
Start with drawl advice helps
Flick allocation information whispers

Start with drawl resist unlocketing
Because be money information whispers
Flick allocation audit nothings

                    TED GREENWALD

Toothpick bone of contention
Don't grace, to whom it may
Doesn't concern you

It concern the plural
Starry airy raiment breathe
Soothing rough road's throat

Maybe have you an idea better
Add local dress to bony sticks
Call attendance, forthwith

Dust in road eyes to follow down
Step off curb say about north
Back beginning slow walk north

Step off curb eyes follow down
Be careful step slow walk north
Back beginning main street manages

                    TED GREENWALD

Words fill mouths
Begin with pronoun mouth
Wordy how it feels

Grammars fill ears
What's that
Heard THAT *right*

Together with words
Fill pronoun with
Dictionary no need

And soon set slide by
With away do wallet size
Same tempto sneeze at nothing

With away do set slide by
Essay alien sneeze at nothing
Same tempto drawn qualms

                                    TED GREENWALD

Step out the door
Trees a crowd
News cheese spread

Use your head
Feels good
The good work

By ear play
Peel down
Watching seem

Step out door hopes on dash
Shall find amongst friends
Night young seat edge

Shall find color hair unearthly
Pay enclose attention seat edge
Night young hopes on dash

                    TED GREENWALD

Bikini countdown
Please scrip
Rumor has it

Something   It hits
No air in here
In each eye, what's

Ashes keep blowback
Bells toll *ings*
Lights on like a light

Same time hold true listen to ebbtide
Become a subtle change out to lunch
For time being recognizable love to buy time

Become a subtle change listen to ebbtide
Next week next year love to buy time
For time being recognizable mea littoral

                    TED GREENWALD

Q and A as bone
Take for grants
People of number worlds

Ribs glow in ribbons
People on the move
Publish moodring studies

Shade with awning études
Move up in the world
Scenic overlook

Remove the same image when get there
Several few remove natural details and pleasant
Customize fail states trees chattery windfalls

Several few remove when get there
Dry and wet food intel pet trees chattery windfal
Customize fail states recognize a future face

Passportless wanders
Mosey into town
Look for kids to kill

Suck on a nation
Alert secret organs
Play media mass oratorio

Now, let's get real
Each soul is branded new
Each nite a long knife

Sounds nice low going away
Tend to overlook they walk among us
Say often enough who else in car

Tend to overlook low going away
Every day never before said who else in car
Say often enough without hesitation pitch

                                        TED GREENWALD

Traffic with emanation tires
Fall in love with n-sides
Figures of speech

Consider yourself one of
Spectators upon a great wall
Pace country from country

Trees' green shoot ashes
Go through in stages
Leaf jingles up on the box

Rustling sounding name talk about getting
Close enough too voices reach rows
Pretty much made footsteps in dirt

Close enough too talk about getting
Get into pants footsteps in dirt
Pretty much made *print it, drano*

TED GREENWALD

A drug form
A prophet doom
The too soon flip

The down drain
A faith article
A novelette

An how suggestion
A then on
The much off

Turnover in   *Hey, got answers*
Pull into lean chance counter
Window down shooing lame excuse

Pull into reach a doorway
Bite inside shooing lame excuse
Window down   *Hey, got answers*

Night slays day
And then some
You know is rotten

Things happen
As then like
How'd you know them

Well is frozen
Who's to say
Believe it's you

Shuddering breath long get over look
Going in or out zinging a skim
Pick a box sip figure fill

Going in or out long get over look
Reel with fishiness sip figure fill
Pick a box leap around string theory

                                        TED GREENWALD

Comes up to me
Say,   *Never heard of*
Meet the real, so

They tell me
Feel as though
Thorough mind lost

Okay, so
Wouldn't move
What's that say

You're saying face friendly
Word mouthing think to tell
That feels good whispery layers

Word mouthing face friendly
Behind back whispery layers
That feels good way like it slice

                    TED GREENWALD

Long gone
Gasp
Make abed

Live across
Table
Work words

Record
Life as
Working flowers

Swing open and shut underbrush lips
Footsteps movie law flex answers
In any case snoop in babbling

Footsteps movie underbrush lips
Flimsy footprints film snoop in babbling
In any case ancient tongues

                                    TED GREENWALD

Say may true
No fair that day
Blood, yum yum

Hear whistle whooo
Make city zoo
Deliver early U

Double form show
Doubly night returns
Embrance no roads

Duck inside light squeeze
Glance over show of hands
Feet slow nail quick

Glance over light squeeze
No pretendo nail quick
Feet slow touch switch

 TED GREENWALD

For keeps calling
You know who
Be very sorry

A soothing because
Too late suggest
Ladder answer

Talk about extras
Yakkety yak
Call lip service

Tongue falls out tape rip off
Kick nothing like tires forget circle everything
Get off phone spill and tear off

Kick nothing like tires so close see bugs
Words drown from hats spill and tear off
Get off phone tape rip off

                              TED GREENWALD

Face says
Where's mouth
Worry   Worry

Deep in thought
Sweetener
Wooly   Wooly

Inner smile
Ring phone
Droopies

Think out loud any thoughts about
Each street get as much out of
Break across a face over idea

Each street any thoughts about
Good as anything moonlight over idea
Breaking a face oozing morons

                                          TED GREENWALD

Grief shoals
Shoulders cry
Taxi   Taxi

Short bus turns
Inland
Everest cards

Suck suck
Ambition nurse
Break allover

Tells you what I know echo in fears
Place and time fall into hands
Home and away point out until

Place and time echo in fears
In same at same point out until
Home and away explain why how

                    TED GREENWALD

Can't see
Indivisible
Camo clouds

Can you *spots*
Five animals
Come back to

Smiling mouth
Dark-op boobs
La rue nips

Feature fracsicle angle heaven praisin
Later hope motor decide in shades
Last second at last reap begin will

Later hope motor angle heaven praisin
Desire consume possess reap begin will
Last second at last float away hindsight

                        TED GREENWALD

As I'm saying
So said
Boom, that's it

You'll never guess
Vision clouds
Hey, check out

On the way out
The dump
Near the end-cap

Mooch written broadcast if said all goes
Invisible barely film at very least
Once-over allover least all agree

Invisible barely film up in said air
American night least all agree
Once-over allover if said all goes

                                        TED GREENWALD

Onionate skyline
Population opinion
Companion pin cushion

Hem   Haw
Just don't freak out
Mr. Peanut par ici

Breathe your elastic
Broken into empires
Hysterical amor accomplice

Get hit with O$_2$ pitch indelible footprints
Everything even is to bumper
History crime bumper doubling

Everything even is early life pass
Everywhere where else bumper doubling
History crime indelible footprints

                              TED GREENWALD

Always little voice
Don't tell me what
Make big to-do

Make a to-don't
Skin crawls
Before skin walks

Zombies
Just ignore them
They go bye-bye

What's to don't like yet do yet
Report say there to listen
Fair to say look through

Report say dub magic grace
Interest in ackage look through
Fair to say yet do yet

                    TED GREENWALD

Not right since
Haven't been
Separate amplifier

World goes to shit
Money multiplier
Happy-be resonator

A half park
Answers to Eve Arden
Babbling brooks

So goes nation voice can't place
But they don't tree leaves only
As saying goes all day long

But they don't put self phone in
And if do all day long
As saying goes voice can't place

                    TED GREENWALD

Infectious laughter
Opportunity (of)
Come as who goes

In contraption who are
In tone (of)
The body's there

Table elementary
Lean periodically
Alert thitherish

While circle square hint not from
Goes without saying reasonable doubtless
Heart in mind probable because

Goes without saying building collapse
Press conference probable because
Heart in mind hint not from

　　　　　　　　　　TED GREENWALD

Worth believe
Your lying eyes
Listen

Someone someone
You know, off
Tells off

Cloudy
Vapor and vaporee
Ding

Likely, *um*, and *um* found what
Always never not not others
Stream concerning note things

Meant to and told so
Be under attack note things
Stream concerning found what

                        TED GREENWALD

That person's me to
Maybe me three
Don't ask

See the picture
And they're like   *Oh*
No one on floor

Heading into a head
Wind down
Isn't going down

Can't won't be sure land mine lines
Elbow room so few ans
Volumes public many ques

Elbow room connective tissue
More than before many ques
Volumes public land mine lines

                          TED GREENWALD

A little menu
Three entries
A stranger

First things
First   Smile
That you?

You go to
Get to
Understand

Light head head thinking line
Next words leaking out *ide*
Through rain enter hearsay

Next words circle
Same with enter hearsay
Through rain thinking line

 TED GREENWALD

Sublime early spin
Isn't that wild
A betrayal altar

Eat with no hands
Lead in, eating with a tie
The fork is introduced

Spoon river la di da
Sound your own yum yum
Hand cup the nearer ear

Complete transfer developments unfold
Other tools science beside word spoken
Too late for so right now

Other tools science wonder desire
Turn allegedorily so right now
Too late for developments unfold

Wear thin smile
Base on fact
Eely shadows

Weather translate
Slate clouds
Good (shake

Head)   Hands
The money
She is no

Star permission giving *why, oh why*
Hold in front heard that
Walk here out one before

Hold in front may explain
Publicity celebrity one before
Walk here out *why, oh why*

                                     TED GREENWALD

Personal lights within
Each word without
A thought thought

Entrance platform
Various moves from
Ramp up exit

Cross out
Think over
More crossout

Laugh then cry reds underneath
Strip away veer slip off with
Minute to minute scene translates

Strip away veer flesh fleshes out
Fingers oments scene translates
Minute to minute reds underneath

                         TED GREENWALD

Claim to snow light
Sway election
Sound with moves

Turning sidewalk
Farm move to town
As a setting

Lines main streets
Up to removable skyliner
Off it and up a ways

Be seen spread out hold and direct
Loom smoke activity surround
Seam comes undone eyes point

Loom smoke pat pat
Legs linger eyes point
Seam comes undone hold and direct

                          TED GREENWALD

Okay, so, I'm not saying
The point is what can happen
So, let's make money word

The road an elbow bends
About a smile down
Stop by, learn more

Shoulder muscles welcome
Walkway one-side
Lingo green wallpaper

Spine attention within hours
Believe painting speaks mistakes for
Posture odds ticket slow embrace

Believe painting closing weeks
Make up mind ticket slow embrace
Posture odds within hours

 TED GREENWALD

Really teeny mouth
Talking about things
Temp take in account

The weather turns
Know what hit you
From our corner

Won't don't need
This way   This way
Let me put it to

Little more strength   *There?*
Pull back mind entrance
Gaping hole trancelike mood

Pull back   *Over here*
Layaway trancelike mood
Gaping hole   *There?*

                                    TED GREENWALD

Barely forgotten
End loony
Make a leg

The letters shape
It looks
Look at how

Don't get wrong
Think it means
Accidental read

Do nothing to it else about it
That this, blah blah throw caution to
Take a subject memoir in end

That this, blah blah about it
Beneath surfettes memoir in end
Take a subject else about it

                                        TED GREENWALD

Cradle smile con solo
Go child gurgles
Morse robots toppling

Look around Sue
Bring back the people people
Deliver baby heart

Sleeps in baby face
Heart shape *rocks*
Handwrite versional

Seeing's believing walk, chew gum
As shall see one road apiece
Coulda went down yonder

As shall see land bags
Get the idea, you, down yonder
Coulda went walk, chew gum

                    TED GREENWALD

Knows scent
Gaping
Gloss a lily

Too why
Teetery
Halo-ize

Base on
Assume snow
What's with this

Hand in truth rhapsody wax rap wane
Frequent shower miles with strings attack
Lend helping sociably leaflike

Frequent shower miles play by products
Clean up after sociably leaflike
Lend second helping rhapsody wax rap wane

TED GREENWALD

Verbal noun shield
Some chromo gammas
Tapis forethought

A no when a yes
Maybe a maybe
Throw out first baby

Trot out a swamp
Nature, suddenly
Elastic utterance

Step-by-step instructions clue's house
Spell end nor less that
Step traces no more than that

Spell end cats doubtless
Sounder out no more than that
Step traces clues' house

　　　　　　　　　　TED GREENWALD

There's a no
Knock knock
Stop yonder

Become toxic
Otherwise fail
Recent attempt

Loosen tie
Define *tight*
Ponder boom

Feel like ties between possible
Is as was as to why
Almost taste very still

Is as was joist poisonal foist
Or wouldn't very still
Almost taste ties between possible

                    TED GREENWALD

Look out my window
See it costs a song
Bye bye hooks, bye bye

Which way Clarksdale
Have a head headache
Never shut up hours long

Merch bell is ringing
Folks enter a tint bing
Folks be right back

One big heart broken radar switch on
Bring back whose asphalt
No empty seats out into street

Bring back appear during
Avenue by far out into street
No empty seats radar switch on

                    TED GREENWALD

Know what I'm saying
Throw in the key
Turn out your lights

Lie down
Do your time
Smile when you say

The verdict comes down
Where big dogs meet
The late great

Message sent out despite many *but*
Mirror bell should don't walk
Glance shows for reasons state

Mirror bell no one said so
At once possible for reasons state
Glance shows despite many *but*

                    TED GREENWALD

Morning appoints said pen
Here to wherever
Bell curves in distance

Line add up to sum
Paragraphs are paging
Get up go to a piece

Down the road a piece
Descends in garment
Sleep with woven names

Secret agent of love tours important spots
Whispers cirrus cloud believe be fictitious
Under old western eyes induce generalization

Whispers cirrus cloud brush up on pony tail
Lover's ear induce generalization
Under old western eyes tours important spots

                    TED GREENWALD

Heat discussion
Doors bang
More voices

Twins insinuate
Join as flame
Dial up a fire

Eye waiting
A finger follows
Sounds nice

Wind picks up place mike
Guy walks past pull over
Afterward see more friends

Guy walks past dumpster downshift
Says *quatre amis* see more friends
Afterward place mike

                    TED GREENWALD

What to read
Precede forsythia
Calendar spring

Directions inside
Fro grain
Before fog rain

Amulet mules
Shlep   Shlep
Nearly tree

List preference order after arrival
Rapids rafters nice thoughts
Thing to do, go to, in fact

Rapids rafters fall underneath
More to come go to, in fact
Thing to do after arrival

                              TED GREENWALD

Snow flake
Crime scene
Suspicion

Try explaining
None for
Appear melt

Ceiling eats
Gotcha
Next move

Twig end at *pop pop*
Ray on what want to say can't believe luck
Have idea too (unguarded moment)

Ray on what want to say word up
Do not drive far unguarded moment
Have idea too *pop pop*

                                    TED GREENWALD

Wait next cloud
Step lively money reader
Adapt to pass for new

Take elevator
Frame wordless mind
Act worthless to throw off

Said to alternate currency
Sign letters with demons
Graphs para meta revisit

Off in sleep name of
Ground open harm Monica self service
Before walk story in real life

Ground open come again
Round about story in real life
Before walk name of

 TED GREENWALD

Line before falling off
Can't rem
Ember stuck gun

Poetry in motion
Walking by beside
Beauty's instrument imperfect

Alphabetical nature
What you take me for
Num num

The laffic it comes it comes
Way back when rants of how
Vocabulary rods looming footage

Way back when don't know how
Take to chagrin rants of how
Vocabulary rods don't know how

                    TED GREENWALD

Tonight with words
Can't be unspoken
Threes a cloud

Before windows is sill
Jump up peer out jump
Looking easy

Forget repeat
Forget myself
Ditto

This is store who sent you
Everyone tells moment wait for
If you listen who sent you

Everyone tells territory for light out
But you got to listen moment wait for
If you listen eludes for the moment

                    TED GREENWALD

Needlepoint episodes
Hard to pinpoint
Can't put put finger

Spendthrift crayola
Circle each scale
Playa weary

New wave inhabits
X-ray blue print
Edifice breathless

Two banana steps useta we useta
Great leap forward bracket entrancement
Death warms over others more become

Great leap forward useta we useta
Learn say *May I* others more become
Death alarms over coulda then went

 TED GREENWALD

Woofing gimme
Bad idea   Bad
But no dog

Temp tee
Lorraine tonight
Is it suppose to

Gotcha shelter
Food clothing
Reduce to

Don't go there stress free
Never went away think what you think
Else to say no big deal

Never went away stress free
Something nothing no big deal
Else to say figure out how

　　　　　　　TED GREENWALD

Stood there
Lower jaw feet
Eyes wide open disclose

Walk through time
Watch to leave on
The evening rush on

O, throw them away
Improved galoshes of spirit
Jangle sink like stone

Deep into floor anything good by
Definitely be listening get a word past
Looks like belonging every perfect anything

Definitely be listening back on a table
Use brain open mouth get a word past
Looks like belonging back on a table

                    TED GREENWALD

For it is kitten
Awake and spend
Should money find you

On or about this day
About, how's there
I'm here   You, where

Matter map making
You better said down
Where am am

Romance in local color lightly over radio
Tailor convenience suit breath lets school out
Done in whole seam they try again

Tailor convenience suit lightly over radio
Say something to me they try again
Done in whole seam not familiar information

                    TED GREENWALD

Lighten up
Word for word
It is written

The world doesn't stop
Take a break
Make or

On note
A real foot
Down look it up

Gift horse mouth no idle threat
Talk a lot about keep *let's* in mind
Sleep windows open no idle threat

Talk a lot about hammer head into twilight
At any given time keep *let's* in mind
Sleep windows open forgotten inalienable

                              TED GREENWALD

Then harder rains
The first word out
This is all before

Feather knock me over
The river's source
First time eyes laid

And before that even
The year before
Old lover sea

All roads lead baby on way
Line tells gone further
In many ways fishing expedition

Line tells does for today
Deep woods fishing expedition
In many ways baby on way

                    TED GREENWALD

Soon to be former
Offer and decline
Show me's and segments

Few who know
Come to light and end
Destruction next line

A commentary running
Alone and for important
Graph solo mondos

Money where mouth, eye look in
Flag where hole utterly, *ah!*, mouth
From hearing say will

Flag where hole index under chin
Knowing say will
From hearing eye look in

                    TED GREENWALD

Desire print it
Foot step in vessels
Long long a go away

Commingle beasts
A dead chest woe
Learn by heart

Between notes, cliffs
Reflection your own
What's in name it

In line with wandering
Tongue hanging tractor con
Backsie frontsie be clause

Tongue hanging recent fingers
Shoe lace be clause
Backsie frontsie wandering

                    TED GREENWALD

Brow wear
See-thru info
If we do something

If we do nothing
Loosen each leaf
Three-hole conclusious

Gathering rulers
Will then lie
Call for night

Standing ovation fits news
Come in overage
Feature life-side *ah*

Come in sweeping miss
So why not life-side *ah*
Feature fits news

                                    TED GREENWALD

Wind picks up
After leaving
Step into lyrics

Humming
Words approx
Seams unravel

Thread save
Breath a match
Walk into

Steam out taken baby steps
Organization be bound by
Can't persuade on roll

Organization   *This means war!*
Be speaking on roll
Can't persuade taken baby steps

Crosshairs on a cheerio
Calls from dispatch
Come in, come in

Tear run down
The battery roads
Rent guns day light

Wear dire straits
If there, there
Terminal tattoo

Take card hardly exaggerate
Lead along councils light come off
Easy for some come back to

Lead along councils mother plays father
Refer destruction come back to
Easy for some hardly exaggerate

                    TED GREENWALD

Say the show
Fork over the road
Looks snow

As they drift
Pile up
Space a day

A fingerprint off
No english
Swipe, strip

Change into in part
Different mind main building
Ashen fusion annex day

Different mind known as
Do about annex day
Ashen fusion in part

                    TED GREENWALD

MOVING PARTS

for Charles and Susan

Look out
Front window
Scene piles
Blue   Blue

Come out of
Look familiar
Front for
Stacks smoke

Speak point
Leave the bike
A busy day

A head
Long arc sights
Dig into

Take a dip
When   When
Enter lately

                    TED GREENWALD

Thrust upon yourself
Over fire place
The olden times
Made up

Little bit softer now
Write furiously
Call on experts
Choppy ring a let's

Sweet nothings
Whispering   Whispering
For crime family only

Eyes only
Out and about
Got get, the idea

Name in future
Reading a little
You *could* say

                              TED GREENWALD

The Book of the Old Days
Fills with beautiful strangers
Almost   *Its* keeping all
Crush to a breast

The on edge
Hairs not a gray gray
Almost   Completely forgot
Fill A

Two takes
Call me in it's the morning
Wind in paper

A language page
Takes down the street
A voice puts a gun at

The back of the neck
Stand hair up and up
Dog nails head this way

                    TED GREENWALD

Moon barely up there
Across the Paris skies
No surprise *don't*
Key represents shift

The door to intent
Plan to starter talks
People disappearing
A little more away

You laff
And then you cry
Imagine how things work

The catch
The pigeon toed the line
Wattage linguine

Arising movie
Happening to me
Only baby goat

                    TED GREENWALD

Actors arrive
The foundling discovery
Two words in a word
Smile detector

Where's the shit
Gonna get me
Assault charge battery
Get have some

Look both ways
Listen to B-side
Dream dip dip

Wouldn't mind
Feel that way
Comes to a heading

The other side on
As the snow
So, flip over

                    TED GREENWALD

Done to knock turn
Pix on muscle memory
Knows too much
Drift over a school

In invisible ink
Documents   *Oh, forget it*
Flatly tat for tat
If as yet an on

Inside all of us
Government adrift
How come, no clouds

Astonishing worker blossoms
Speed bumps into spring
Grass breezes haves

Starter motor
The call the wind ive
Dab like-minds

                    TED GREENWALD

Remove any *oh, too*
Nothing reminds me
Now appears the from to
It's now said

Be head toward
Where's the fire
Time *you wanna level*
You tell me

Mouth is moving
Pity on moving day
Ear to ground links

Use to be pre
Deep pockets
Precede *it's*

The fact wakes us
Got to got to
Restless masonry

                    TED GREENWALD

Following the following
Little known
Try sound out
Rosh sal ber you

Il tleut à verse
Black out in white
Spring slice
Sara Po to ga

Almost personal approx
Nature crying on
The shoulder road

Weather first, what's
So's wouldn't hear of
Strange hair walks

Unbeknownst to
You mean doc
Government (so) supposedly

 TED GREENWALD

The not humans
It is a first step
Much more needs
What is to be done

Opinion chocolate cherry
With liquidated centers
Still applies, fills out
Feel at, in the then

Day up in the crayons
For next hour be true
Fork take stage right

A continuance stays
Walks on set to walk off
Blanket as a play film

It's anybody's guest
My guess is somebody
Unfolds like a *baby baby*

                    TED GREENWALD

Busy work flowers
Allocute to
Whose spring is
The drive-by snow

Common wheels define
A perfect storm
Interlocking factotums
May a bee

Lie against own faces
A phasing out
What's with the breeze

Leave wind shadows
Another day bump into
As was as was

Keep coming up
Repossess shaving points
All of the above

                    TED GREENWALD

Heat often off
Talk warm and friendly
A great smile
Live-in now now

Legend lonely life
Doors throw open
Over the heart's plate
Over and over yer out

Car door dust message
Bike wheels sound leaves
Air's a solid

Insides meet insiders
Meandering worth considering
Your weekly reader

Comparative snow
Running into to collate
Doubletake park no more

                    TED GREENWALD

Enter invisible
Exit under a cloud
Just sitting around
Logic tesselations

Forever never say
So, why now
Trees bark is worsted
Suite with shore's suit

Scientifically formulate
How you say
Free your body

Love for hundreds years
And count on
Fingers, all ears

The have-nots
The half hitch
The sheetbend

                              TED GREENWALD

Chiclet choo choos
No telling who's who
No gamblers no ramblers
But keep the trains

Put away your fortune tellers
Greatest thing seen
The mind cleans up
Immortalize in solinoid

A gem
Gotta dash help
With your mouth open

Street ink cred
Capsules a gel
Goes (without) saying

To-ing and froing
Wing don't mind if
And if I don't

　　　　　　TED GREENWALD

Squirrely comma
Close
The inner door
And open

The outer door
The other body
Lies next
Believe you me

Now sayings
Lapping waves of idiots
Sing Stalin's praises

Hair raising Lenin
Sun shines from above
Marks barn burn down

Rising vanity mercury
As grave me send
Snow likely

                        TED GREENWALD

Shrug off deep snow
This close   This close
Word now comes
Close with cold calls

Visitor come over
Like you mean business
Lips missing mouth
Painting on a camel

It's the streets
Looking at each other
You do the math

There's talk the face with
Cry out
Turn around

Run up to the sky
That's *cold cold*
And election coming up

 TED GREENWALD

Slip ring into phone
Scientists see new coal saw
Roam and seizures
Catwalk clouds lamplit gaslight

Knowing the way deep down
See heard felt
Talk in particles, small
Bud wit twigs

Nah
Gotta get
Can't get

Lemma git
Aromatic
Direct molecules

Lead
Corollary lemme
Hasp pit fall

Checkpoint unseen hand
Give imps the yips
Growing body of bodies
Likens to a rock

The whom to
Before come along for irony
Revelation solver trains
People just kinda

Legal tender cooler
Back rooms despise
Bring your own hinges

Upon Xing
Answer in between lies
Use more once

Word paint by numbers
Swamp grass wavering
The oaf of office

                    TED GREENWALD

True presto digits
A lotto big money
Why'd you say it
Talk to your doctor

Once more glows
Theses and thoses
Left off pave way
Each your turn reveals

High din
Handle on this hour
Weird neighbor

Seems normal
Spin in big low
Cloud shadows walk chow

A way of life
In propaganda world
On a ball

                    TED GREENWALD

Clouds of undoing
There but not there
Pond swimming duck tape
Anyone walks by

On edges union squared
The surface of the sun
Do nothing else to it
Accumulate multipliers

Street lights
Come on up
A waste of time

Powerful magnify
Light who hair
Stands up somewhere

Long way around
Don keys
The five burros

                    TED GREENWALD

Door knocks turn
Cinnabar mental
Car face electoral twong
One a dose light

The old you the pick up
Take an objection
Carry out carry away
Line least

The more there is to like
Like what we like
Know the more we like

Like the more we like
Leaves by Stalin's satin
Grass waves wave back

Where the buffalo roam
A nickel everyone's for
Turn on once upon a dime

                                    TED GREENWALD

Y O Y
The dog is happy
A precarious time
A young bear's life

Isoceles testimonial
Icicles
Proceeds go to *the*
Anything doing

Wear as tiny print
Eats dog while serving
Brand new demurs

Their own coffee drive-thru
Tired they R R they
Out there somewhere

Haven't stop for weeks
The who's asking eh
A discovery jungle

Each stroke
Pen touch down
Spoken in tongues
Open a crack

Passing
Wheel within wheels
Somedays, poof
Untying

Dollar fell sighing
Against the yen
Inhabit dream more wan

—had to —had to
He said she said
Laugh cry makes think

Oh, first stage, drop off
Travel many houses
But, first things second

                    TED GREENWALD

Pan go gold
A sell aroma
A letter house
Wear a home

Double as feature
Slaves no visitor
Fall when so disin-
Gracious shadow grate

My steamed associate
A sadly deepness
Scene of unfold

Compos pathos homegrown
Lego of everything
Put up with the river

Itself is singular
Loop on the outs
Make no interiors

                    TED GREENWALD

The late hamburger
Allow for aloe
A windy sometimes
Change mastermind

Won't just won't
Go away (go away)
Make speech *very*
Late-day burgerish

So good read slow
Accident blocking Elaine
Distant squirrel curlicue

Entreaty varieties
Babies ah-ah
It's nice……but…

It's been goodbye so long
Fly in the face of reasons
For want of upon light fits

                    TED GREENWALD

An airtight alibi
Airing, dim thing
Oh, *come on!*
Tech photos scene

Protect blueprints
Contemplate multiplex
One a way up
Backwards at something

Drop kiss deadly
Clip coupon to New York
Changeling into history

Figure out figuring out
Return to moonbeam
Road be not concern

Something for say-so
Sound light me to whom
Undo a finale it may

                    TED GREENWALD

There's gonna be any shooting
Men go mad
It's a journey
Gotta get my rest

Facts on the ground genre rinse
Stake high, hot dogs law
A good great hook
Think count on fingers

Down book
So smoky
A single mom

Make ends meet
Well-means forget
Call for friendly

An opinion
An opening near
Fan's fanzine

 TED GREENWALD

Be a similar boat
In a sameness sea
Extra billowy cloudy
Off and on a napkin

In doctored no
Return to vegetation
The same however
List in breeze

Twisted, yet, methodical
As if readings a form of
Surge chatter erase out

Record ether or nether
Rereproduce ininform
And still they still come

Talkies unidentify
Memory dies abbreviator
Sold as ass truth baby live

                    TED GREENWALD

Get out there and focus
Throw voice into box
Let me out, let me out
Believe our understanding

Extend a friendly and
In cash to an *or*
A punctuation curvature
Indigenous specific sites

If burger answers for
Give a chance
For all noice heard

Put it to right
People in place things
Askly the tough questions

Heard once so he say she say
Key chain
Be yonder, words

    TED GREENWALD

Come as you are
What the fuck kind of dog
Out of the way go
Those who know

Scratchoff ministers
Mint borderless tensions
Tongues wag mesmerize
Unnotice far from flung

Same over
But still…
Gonna am

Touché
Left felt
Really something

Specks use
And over
Sulky

                    TED GREENWALD

Put the top down
From the bottom up
Airy notices
Join today

Science on the march
Date with a needle
Mind, what's on
Without saying

Our little secret
An easy fool
Memo saying

Can say the same
Still like *new*
Water on anybody

Fix light funny name for
The *just* anybody
Shutters blabby

                    TED GREENWALD

Great towel shift
The line too long
Tease is oolong
Every little word bigger

Wide open more trees
Walk from seconds
The smile on a face
Rhythmic reading writing

In tellings
Lost in mists
With a scene

Boss in the back
Sleeping
Fingernail drops

Wind blows tree
Shadow dog
Salad days camera

                    TED GREENWALD

Tech's our friend
Feel deep the keystone
Save space save time
Mind drive you crazy

Model out
Not a shadow of a forma
Save continuum
There have been nights

Lemon limelight
Drifts ask how
We told you so

Need you need
Like you do
Mono logue what chenille

With waffles
Ivan the terrible 2s
Mind as of hair

                    TED GREENWALD

And good?   *So* good
Just so, too
Miss no detail
Moon sidesteps sun

Shush, right, get it
Happiness no squares
Twice-told two timers
Pretty pretty mumbo combo

Going in hot
Oh, phone a graph
Slightly anointing sax

Spread out proteins
Toss comes up retail
Expect, *won't happen*

Know with knowing
Sit in the longest yard
Stovepipe happy horseshit

          TED GREENWALD

So now told
Good of all
Past prelude to qua
Subtract the nails

A grow ling sense
Please, don't get me start
Fool by like us
News self-sung standards

Guy behind the guy
Taken aback
The music behind the music

Get arms around
Tourist falls to death
Just ice vaporizer

On sum hair
Will come of it
Drink soft minutae

                    TED GREENWALD

Things get weird
You're in a place
Pass pixie window
Winter in an elbow

Sick of drizzly shit
Bad weather thing
Think time to book
The lost you yous

Know much then of
If there's anything
Don't hesitate

Not lighteners within
Who you know
Very 50s   Very Jackie

Hit rewind running
Safe houses
No safe beds

                    TED GREENWALD

Roam the earth
Downshift, go north
Garment a nerve whodunnit
Step back to view

Repeat air
With each shoulder
Goes to the heart
No strings

Ah, so this is
Nature
How unnatural

Seed insurance for
Nearly closely
Away for raining

Get off the train
Money at it
Runaround soothe

                    TED GREENWALD

Long story short
The greater the simplifiers
For those of you (like me)
Wrap with legend acquifers

Border a desperate country
The city of the future
Shake well
Collapse terriers

While supplies last
Look left
You looking person

Really   Really
Great ass
Maybe, not so great

Do for now
See yourself with
Can't turn away (can't)

                    TED GREENWALD

A city upon a pill
More likely be correct
Or say we do
Or say we do

Why do birds sing, so gay
Better part breaks day
Change with purchase
Only is not dead

Sleepers tell their story
Angels on angle irons
Spruce up shoe trees

Unknowing moves in
Suffering no nowadays
Gives glance within reasons

Put head on shoulder
Within listening distance
Sleep freely public

                    TED GREENWALD

Like a hand
Arm to the teeth
Chord why so long
Make official

Convoy movies on
Wherewithal do so
Classroom too too
Few few befores

News broke
Law of the buzz
You know, it's like

Breeze with motors
Ultimate goal, *better*
See album

See be seen
By-word no problem
Can go afar

                    TED GREENWALD

Been about shoulders
Nice for five notes above
Here   Ask being question
And here   Said be there

Airplane runway aprons
A street thing, a sweet thing
Bleeve, follow upon
Your foetus, your fire

Leak in other words
A goof with piss
A person of interest

Bullets step out
Stuck to thematics
A dog in a novel

Because because at crisses
In direction of flight
Okay with it

                    TED GREENWALD

We'll get back
Call never comes
Bridges unfold
O phone gonna be

Know full *well*
Half well pebble deep
Reverb plot pulls
Open loan noun

Leading the movie
Still good friends
Talk each day other

Up in the Poconos
Mountains and shit
A day-brightener

A friendly welcome
No picture needs
Be seen what

                    TED GREENWALD

Real live speakers
Real live talks
Faint breeze
Borrow skin

Edit, abridge sway
On the way down
Back in day
Live that shit

But the law won
But no one knows
Exactly   Y

Glow is there
Wow, but
Swirling leaves

Pall ever so
A hard look
Giving away

                    TED GREENWALD

Star's dire
It's anybody's business
Tap dancing on the phone
Wear alligator clips

Waitress serves up disk
A hope pin butterfly
Redemption embed
Green stamps cast die garage

Before the fact
We bid farewell
We take with us

Just stop me
Rueless
The only idiot

Run, don't walk
Whoever is them
Kind of, west of

Shape an envelope
Sketch on a napkin
The scheme of things
Such and circumferences

Lives in circumstances
Some part true
Legs cross lips the word
Back, then a living forward

A crazy day
After a
Not so crazy day

But, wait
If you call now
Broad brushstroke

But, wait
Slippery news cycle
Freak goes cc's

                                  TED GREENWALD

Snappy glasses
The ayes have
Deliver now believe
The ads run

Grasp for air
Muffin thin arms
Way wrong rubs
Oxygen subtitles

According to testimony
Nothing with wires
Money to make (lots)

An empty this
Is, was, so
Talk about what who

A city known
Nothing quite makes
Quite as a snow

                    TED GREENWALD

This is a dream, right?
The eyes some tooth
Along for shadow ride
Am I reading it right

Pass through a needle
Fuck off, before and since
With each dream call
Meeting place paragraph

Guinevere of tix
Sharp blades
Foot hits (oboe) shore

Unique as a fingerprint
By just show timing up
Along doing been

Moment to be in
Breadcrumb trail
Tastes like chicken

Luftmensh mouthfeel
Exec sleight hand
Us in decision
Dawn is pre-mourne

Digitize norm personal
Role moving forward
Source notes ice
Keyring keeps raining

From the original
Grasp itineraries
Gasp wire diagram

Thank you for listening
Things *to do* that travel
Snow falls moment

Seen through rain's disguise
Only sounds not english
Sun bolo lookout

 TED GREENWALD

Tell you what
I'm gonna do
Don't stop for nothing
On a hill

Start transparency
Form a government
Mother tears recall
Gonna do for you

Darkening with swallows
An echo lake
Crossroads

Creep to sleep words
The word for
A word resin

Amber alert
Fly on wall eyes
Be a guess

                    TED GREENWALD

Foam mental voices
Read into writing
Petty hard eight dreams
Get on all petit-fours

Bus passes
Keep on versus Gs
Nights in row
Re-memorize traffic

Would be over soon
Dawn of sometime
Children playing

And, hey, order today
The went pun
One more Kim

Use wisely, do try
When and so on
What'll it be like

                    TED GREENWALD

Dig into deeper if
Something to chew on
Go on umbrella balance
Facts sweep away

A leg stand on
Eye history close
Sickens to think
Walks of the unwell

It's…it's not a game
Sales pitch write
Align with *this is history*

Border through verbs
A connection so
Not to say something

No need to know
Story sand fingertips
Talk nice to the tiger

                    TED GREENWALD

Rules pro rubs
Lying down *or*
With street cred
Cross burnt offering

Howlin' wolf wind
Lantern in mouth
Come to things
Ignore glue rhythm

Fear cupola
On true luck
Today goes light

Deep freeze all in
No standing
Loading and unloading

Melt into snow dentine
Have me some fun
Tributaries

　　　　　　　　TED GREENWALD

Jump on
The fans know
To do with something
To-do list

Deepish smile
Clothesless
Gravity's subtlety
Ford ruby icon

A prophet at loss
History's laptop dance
Nothing on paper

The point yon lucky
What must be seen
Passes this way for

Makeover sop
A running cat
Space between lottas

                    TED GREENWALD

Droplets
Translucent shoulder
Read over
Midair notes

Triplets
Personally, doubt it
Looks as though
(Describe *though*)

Say no more
Draw toxin outta
Can-do be said

It ill end
Business as unusual
Iliad laudanum

Wireless cuts
Back in the day
Too this too that

TED GREENWALD

Starve connotones
Look it, look up
The moon
Else is news PR

It's the moon shine
Con not star
Cease to be simply
Tell the reps

A coming attraction
Walk together
Same footsteps

In our hats
Said period
Comma impersonations

Along riddance
Smell fries
Ride down

          TED GREENWALD

Go bump
Slump over a wheel
Car's park
Nerve mess

Chimes ring
Storm sobbing
Scary music
Sorta tai chi

Run eye over
The more sense
Head count easy

Mai tai
Star due
List under heading

Friends stay friendly
Stretch legs
Tide of warranty

TED GREENWALD

The dumping of the cash
She be out there somewhere
Drive around in money shapes
Look hither then yawn

Rayon terrier tag sale shine
Noodling byways unanimus verbs
Stomach rub anything actually said
Ice dice to be did done

Streets saying
Food in units
Slotted evening

Explains, see spoon
High life amputate
Read the book

Labs appears
Smiling in yellow
Define coats

TED GREENWALD

Whisper fence
Rush the week
Pompom moralizing
Rara, say standees

Demiurge the team on
Inside ept script
It's a mental thing
Destination stands for

Really do feel
Interest in becoming
All included

Take interest
Many others on
List half experience

Same same place
A similar tree
Under simile

                         TED GREENWALD

The next shoe shoes
Drops
Rain raindrops
A nobody knows

Be her bald she be
The as crow flies
Theme song envelopes
Pear designate

Dollar water lilies
Exchange services and good
To eat in order

Nothing is happiness
Ever been in life
Be they like homies

Look up clouds
Said so in reports
Very dish from nature

                    TED GREENWALD

Do-over dew
Where grass is greener
Good news goes bad
Canopy blows off

Mail's semi screwy
With *it's rain*
Hour dress minutes
Van troubles does it give

Talk the night through
The complete picture
Anyone else around

A small chance dance floor
Come in during meat time
As soon as heard

Look like you listen
Figure out someone says
Why telling me this

                    TED GREENWALD

Cloud of knowing
Links gleam
Morning goes over
Alive with weather

Anything in writing
Sheepdog goofy
Burger plays ketchup
Eye corner

Hear a voice
Lighting the mood
Air warm

Mustard been a reason
Gets you thinking
At tempera, no say

Currency milling around
A mom intersection
A mini-now marquetry

　　　　　　　TED GREENWALD

Hands of an artist
Shoot the strangled pianist
Leap from silver scream
Come in at the knees

Hopes dim sum
Grace, as a friend
Have to do with it
Stare at pair a dice

Flies the eaten crow
Passes for past
Whole truth about

There will come a time
Seeing lines
Shadowy world of

Glance and smile
Easy motion
Chip in a tree

                    TED GREENWALD

Dog smile
Finally done
In lieu of
Scream peak

Don't ask
No telling
Small room
Alongside

Tell who how
Whistle
Echo quick hello

Keepsake tracks
All in life
Sleep be put in

Fall back on
If you say
Talk in undertones

                    TED GREENWALD

Footfalls *as*
Small wonder
Go on for years
Frog cog

Listening, uh
It's like leaving
Things happen
In a way

Forever yours
Slice into mind's eye
End of the day

Take to meds
Taking to bed
What police saying

Walk back toward
Fond frond
Fat man smokes

                    TED GREENWALD

Leave open the road
For nothing else
Especially nice
Be brought about as

Beg in ham medium
A pinch for some if
Can't figure
Take that next step

Start out driving snow
Read the little words
Thanks to top donor

Milky way outstrips Candy Bar
Clamor for money damages
Defectors, eye out for

Walleye official *papieren*
Believe in glimpse driveby
Accident contrivance kill

 TED GREENWALD

Never this the day
Is thereness tenderness
Word made obsoletion
Any given take

Killer friday good
The mind of the waiter
Square roots doing the tapioca
Tanks for tapes

Stop and smell
The supposes
Still of the night

Drive around so swell
Tuff issues
Crush as strange terrain

Euphemism munition
Fire into crowd
Afar on cities

                    TED GREENWALD

Dust settles muscle places
Deep air, grass
A plain fringe
Weekday someday change into

Bridges flesh out
The road to infinity
Finding go about, no further
Things for a jones

It's winter
But in the fall
Summer isn't over

Even yet, yes
The winter's spring
Can only mean

One thing
Snow's on way
Foggish, looking rain

　　　　TED GREENWALD

Simple radio goop
Ode twixted
Airport cookout cut
Slipper bam

Retread diss tribulation
Music dark future
Launder money white
Knucklehead cognates

A proven fac
Inside the country
Nothing worse

Roll around morning
Feeling as always
No choice but call

A big thing to ask
Tap timetable foot
Nexus in a hoodie

                    TED GREENWALD

Aroma ectomy
Pour heart into
Eyes pull up
Don't get out

Easy but echo-y
Marquee abesques
Video wide following
Virgin long looker

Bell curve cries
No one home
Suck on a claw

Clear day dog gone
Cover with a fib
Use car to dumpling

Knock head against
A wall flower
Range is fence

                    TED GREENWALD

Solid states creep unto
Cloud is a small bag
Line story boards
Tell their story side

Shaky, mainly goofball
Hairline shoreline
Bend downturn around
Obviously, some getting

A great message
A simple message
About the breath

A better person makes
A way of life
Be on your way

Bigger things in life
Goes back to body
Deep fried precincts

                    TED GREENWALD

Comes next
Said all along
Bowling for djellabas
Lonely cool breeze

Climb stares
Breathlike freshets
Over and out life forms
Ghoul list pronounce

Snake eyes
Lights come up
Read through

How wanna feel
Not want nothing
None lost

No qualms
Actually not only
About opening

                    TED GREENWALD

Conversational embroidery
On the something or other
Live in a new error
With heavens onerous

Human chain letter
Actual length nothing species
Nothing here suggests
Knife cuts a fork

Quick, duck
In a row
Transitory money

Live-in city
Sentence end
Suspicions

Value clue
Way some do
Sum of our gears

TED GREENWALD

A person familiar with
The talks, walks
On as an over
Tinkling piano pee

Location location location
Last of days
Loco runs out of
Halo mechanical cuts dash

As I look back
As I live and breathe
As one among many

As many as you want
As good as gone
As the bridges sing

As seen on tv
As another way of life
As I look forward to

                    TED GREENWALD

Ted Greenwald was born in Brooklyn and raised in Queens. He is the author of over thirty books, including: *Clearview / LIE* (United Artists, 2011), *3* (Cuneiform Press, 2008), *Permanent Record* (LRL, 2008), *In Your Dreams* (BlazeVox, 2008), and *Two Wrongs* (Cuneiform Press, 2007), a collaboration with Hal Saulson.

Made in the USA
Monee, IL
07 July 2026